ODE TO SOPHIE

A COLLECTION OF POEMS

AABHA ROSY VATSA

This book is dedicated to my third baby

Sophie

Contents

Contents

Preface

I have loved animals since the day I read the children's classic BLACK BEAUTY by Anna Sewell. I recently read a very special book, THE DOGTRINE OF PEACE by Dr Manjiri Prabhu. In my review of the book I had expressed my fondness for animals, especially our dear pet labrador Sophie. So much so that I mentioned her twice in my recently published book, AMIDST THE SUNFLOWERS : Letters To My Grandchildren.

Long, long after I am gone, long long after Sophie is gone we will be immortalized together.

When I read about the Ukranian techie woman who carried her aging twelve and a half year old German Shepherd on her shoulders and walked 17 kms to flee Ukraine, I was deeply moved.

I felt I too needed to show some TLC to my sweet Sophie.

So after putting my two babies on the cover of my poetry books, it was now time to pamper my third baby. Sophie has given the Midha family so much love from the very first moment we saw her.

So I compiled together my 30 poems and self published the book, and voila ODE TO SOPHIE !

#AGiftForSophie

Preface

1. THE REBIRTH

She gasped in disbelief
It was shocking, the text on her monitor
What was even more debilitating, the voice on the phone
An aborted ending
To what could have been a victorious triumph?
She gulped and swept aside the tears
Her body began to grow limp
And her tongue felt like a piece of over used leather
The devil had won
Again and again
And again today
As she lay comatose
The maid came in, bringing a box of sweets
Ma'm please eat this, gudiya brought
Stunned at this unexpected gesture
She picked up a Haldiram mithai and ate it
Dejected, she unfriended several people
And then came the rebirth
Once, twice, thrice, a fourth time.
Lavish praise
Warm words of appreciation
And above all an open declaration of love from a close one
The devil may have won yet again

But there was still goodness left on earth
Tiny miracles of hope
God's manifestation through his messengers
She wiped her tears
This time tears of joy
And welcomed her rebirth
Yet again.

2. GOOD VS EVIL

Life the alluring and mysterious mistress
Rolling out a plethora of deeds
Every moment erasing emotions restless
Skillfully pricking out prickly weeds
The sinner lazily saunters along
Unmindful of the lusty road
Singing a loud broken song
Uncaring of deciphering life's secret code
The philanthropist takes a leisurely walk
Gently sowing seeds of harmony
Going all the way in walking the talk
Singing an incredible sweet melody
The twin faces of the human mind
The sinner and the philanthropist simply entwine
The journey meanders into alleys blind
Dreaming of a life bordering on shine.

3. FRIENDSHIP

One fine day we met by chance
The Sun was bright and the heavens danced
We decided to walk hand in hand
And share our lives in a manner grand
The ups and downs of life may come
But you my friend are a dear chum
We can sit under the stars and laugh
And swear loyalty on each other's behalf
Friends are a gift we give ourselves
A nectar so sweet that always excels
So let's make merry and enjoy the ride
For you are my dear friend and my pride
Today on friendship day I say an earnest prayer.
That no matter what we always care
May all the lord's blessings be bestowed upon you
Your friendship is more beautiful than the tender dew.

4. WHEN LOVE ARRIVES

When love arrives truly, it is overpowering. Totally unexpected, like a bolt from the blue.Titilating a million unimaginable emotions in you. It can only happen when the divine blesses, for you meet so many people in life, but that one special one sweeps you off your feet. You meet good people, attractive people, successful people, generous people, inspiring people but the spark of true love happens only once in a lifetime, with divine grace. And when love arrives, it brings with it an ache for fulfillment, for shared moments, longing, intimacy and the inescapable heartache. And should there be a long parting, love makes one a poet, giving way to the deepest expressions of intimacy. For when love arrives, it parks itself eternally, never ever to retreat.

5. MAGIC

It arrived out of the yonder blue
A love totally unexpected like a fluttering butterfly emerging from the chrysalis
Sweeping aside the melancholy in a bear hug
Spreading a carpet of million dreams
Everything turned to shimmering molten gold
There was a nip in the air
As if Spring had arrived in mid Autumn
Oh, it was magic and nothing else
Because it triggered a river of unending joy
A permanent ecstasy in the heart
That none could ever dare to steal
It was nothing less than a colossal blessing
The magic of Spring in mid Autumn!

6. A LITTLE PARADISE

Nestled among the row of houses
Adjacent to the fitness park
Is a 'Little Paradise'
Where the sound of flute plays in the street
The tender coconut vendor calls loudly
Just as the sugarcane juice vendor tinkles the bell
The portable idli dosa vendor plays his recorded message
While the vegetable vendor sells till the wee hours of the night
The blush rose pink room is home to paintings
Two Ganeshas silently blessing the house
The youthful monk paintings fills the house with unparalleled spirituality
Echoing the vibrations of the backyard mandir
The wild lilac walls speak of dreams and desires
Offset beautifully by the Banaras ghat painting
A mask here, a dream catcher there
Miniature serial paintings and a message of 'The Simple Life'
The satin blue walls welcome a quiet peace
Just as the photos of Ma, Pa, Nana , Nani
And a vivid 50th wedding celebration collage
Bring alive the true owners of this "Little Paradise'
The bhagwa colored wall beautifully offsets the OM painting

Just as the quadrant Mahamrtunjoy mantra defies death
And the refurbished dining chairs in deep rose velvet
Beckon guest for a hearty meal
The front verandah is the juxtapose of commotion
A witness to the excited pre Diwali crackers by eager kids
While the snakelike plants in colourful planters
Bow in gratitude for a fresh lease of life
The mandir room is the sanctum sanctorum
Guarded vigilantly by the Panchmukhi Hanuman in white and gold
Ma Jagdamba stands tall framed by the crimson chunri
As the devotee squats on the floor to light the five flames
The first floor breathes in silence
Glad to be rid of the evil eye
Silently waiting for the eventual day
It will explode with happy voices
The kitchen elegant in the rose theme
Sighs happily, "This is my happy place'
Happily a mélange of old and new cookware
Even as the prasad is cooked on the fire
The second kitchen hugs old memories
A ray of commodities once in use
Showcasing the wheelchair and the walker of the lady of the house
A silent witness to the sands of time
The adjacent park seems like a friendly courtyard of the house
Pipal, Neem, Jamun, Bilwa, Champa, Guavav breathe happily

The Cluster fig tree extends a heady fruity fragrance of the peach figs
Just as the morning grass is adorned by the fallen Parijat flowers
The rooftop is sheer bliss
Open to the Sky, Sun stars and the moon
Here sitting on the love seat I go in trance
For this 'Little Paradise' is none other than Mum's precious home.

7. CROSSING OVER

The fire threatened to burn like the raging neon green hulk
Leaping crimson tongues of hurt and anger
Sweeping aside in a frenzy, the good that still remained
As shockwaves spread through the mind
The sheer injustice of it all would fan the flames
Threatening to send the fire into quantified smoke
Her heartbeats pulsated with the rhythm of flames
Until calm arose from would have been cinders
Burnt to soot?
She reflected at the inevitable extinction
And then she summoned the genie of goodness
Crossing over, she embraced forgiveness
Relieved at the renewal
For karma would take its own sweet course.

8. JOY

Caught in the intricacies of a swirling quagmire
Is any joy left in life?
At the recieving end of Judas' betrayal
Are there any moments of bliss?
Dreams furiously ruptured and seemingly beyond reach
Will happiness ever play hop scotch?
When the road ahead screams a silent never ending wail
Will the destination ever court the bewildered?
Cascading tears of pain and longing
Will the lotus stand tall above the mud?
But does not the darkest night end in a rapturous dawn
Filling the cosmos with the effervescence of new hopes?
Does the night not serenade the stars and a full moon
Sprinkling its subtle charm on a waiting vegetation?
Do the raindrops not morph into a breathtaking rainbow
Pulling even the old and jaded in a whirlpool of joy?
Does the sinking Sun over the ocean each dusk
Not rise meteorically to a brilliant flame disc?
Does a harsh winter not give way to Spring
Rejuvenating the Earth and making it laugh with joy?
Oh yes, even the stringent of fortunes
Even the darkest of destinies
Even through the burden of Himalayan obstacles

Joy breezes in to the human soul.

9. A ROBUST GIRL

A robust girl with dreams in her eyes
Yet poised to meet fate with a smile
A storehouse of faith and abundance she is
Beauty of youth and grace she is
My little girl who cried at birth
Is now mellow and full of mirth
The dark clouds gathered by droves
But she valiantly said, 'I shove'
A mother's delight oh so pure
A sure shot recipe to smile and cure
She is my little darling all grown up
I pray her life is a brimming cup.

Chapter10

A dew drenched blushing lotus
A concerned offspring
An over generous mate
An unexpected call
A compassionate friend
A benevolent stranger
A divine message
A picture worth a million words
The silken threads of the Lord's presence,
Hope.

11. DUSSEHRA

It is that time of the year again
When every soul claps with glee
As the festival Dussehra arrives in amiable Autumn
Setting the pace of the festive season
Culminating in the festival of lights, Deepawali.
In this materialistic world
With whims and fancy
Karma stands tall
Regal
Elegant
Ethical
Full of integrity
A passport to a blessed life
Delight in Karma
In the exhilarating joy of goodness
In the necessity of dharma as foretold by Krishna in the Bhagwad Gita
In the act of righteousness
Justice
Law
And closure
So on Vijaydashmi
It is the culmination

Of nine nights of celebration of Goddess Durga
Her cosmic dance
As she annihilates the buffalo demon Mahisasura
In the form of Mahishasurmardini
Vanquishing forever the
Darkness
Evil and
Negativity
And all animalistic instincts
As also the burning of Ravana, Meghnad and Kumbhkaran
By Sri Ram
A festival passed down fromTreta yuga to Kalyuga
A celebration of the spirit of Dussehra
The defeat of the mighty ten headed demon
The ultimate victory of
Good over Evil
A lesson every mother teaches her child
For
Satyamev Jayate
Truth always triumphs
Goodness always triumphs over evil
The ultimate and only law of the Universe

12. PRICELESS

You were born for a purpose
A gift of life bestowed by the Almighty
Disregard your doubters
Discover your true potential, for you are priceless
You were born in a family
In a chosen land
On a specific date
So make your mark, for you are priceless
Your journey is your very own
Frought with danger, tyranny, ghouls and demons
It is futile and a waste of time to compare
Rise above the storm, for you are priceless
Your DNA is surely unique
And so is your talent
You can do what no one else can
Believe this, for you are priceless
Remember the Parable of talents?
It is what you do with your destiny
That truly makes your life worthwhile
So rise and shine to unchartered heights, for you are priceless.

13. THE ROSE

When I was just a little girl
And picked my Hindi book and curled
I came across a lovely poem
None other than the Rose and a thorn omen
It was soon time for the Hindi poetry competition
I picked a poem and asked for Dad's approval
Nay, this poem is certainly not the best for the competition
Chose the Rose and a thorn for a result fruitful
So I did as father said
And recited the poem, Rose and a thorn
It was a poem indeed vivid
And impressed the judges and even the Unicorn
Years later I marveled at the beauty of Rose
And life gave plenty of lessons of the thorn
For joy and sorrow are the inseparable cogs of a wheel
Never was a rose without a thorn born
So I decided to embrace this poem of childhood
So eagerly endorsed by father
Sifting through the mazes of life
And the fragrance of Rose I chose to gather
Every facet of life might have thorns
But what matters most is the blossoming Rose
A simple fact of life and nature too

An answer to every dilemma life posed.

14. BELOVED JUNE

June you are infamous for being the hottest month
A month that makes you shudder at times
And wait anxiously for the arrival of monsoons
Certainly not a month to be celebrated
But this year June was different
The vivid blue of the sky brought calmness
Despite the heat it brought a heady clarity
A clarity that had eluded for a decade and a half
What was so special about the winds this year of June 2021?
It baffled me some more
Till it dawned it was nothing but God's timing
Unfolding the clues pure
Beloved June, the eighth day to be precise
Even as I await the monsoons, I shall remember you a lifetime
For you inadvertently solved the riddle that had puzzled me
And miraculously set me soaring in the sky
I am a free bird to take on new frontiers
Dance in the coming rains
Go cascading in the thrilling waterfalls
And run through the pine scented trees of mountains
Beloved June you have become so dear to me
As dear as the month of my birth
While one gave me life

You gave me the celebration of a second life.

15. AGELESS LOVERS

Amidst the humdrum life
Of cooking and cleaning
Checking up on social media
Even as boredom threatens to engulf me
Life, like a promising bloom
You dish out your surprises.
The sheer joy of the unexpected
As goodness engaged a decade ago
Comes knocking at my door
With joy unimagined
Life comes a full circle
And is suddenly full of possibilities
Boredom flung like a discarded tissue
As I revel in the joy of the hour
O life what pretty promises have you got in your magical bag?
Keep sending these little pockets of affirmations
And make me dance to the secret rhythm of the cosmos
Life
I know you and I
Are ageless lovers.

16. I ASPIRE

A day earmarked for women of the world
The whole wide world over
A day when I aspire
To wear freedom like a perfect fit
I aspire that I won't be judged
If I suddenly decide to embark on a career
Where I won't be taken for granted
And my limitations won't be roadblocks
A world where I live free of fear
Of being mobbed in a crowd
Or being stalked on a lonely road
A world where my capacity to give
Won't be exploited
Where my sincere efforts will go down memory lane
In the annals of family and friends
A world where I face no gender discrimination
Where I am asked to handle tasks based on my calibre
Where I can travel solo at any age
And go for walks in the woods
A world where I am treated equal in a marriage
Neither a Hitler nor a saint
One where I can freely voice my thoughts
Without shadows of prejudice

A world where I can explore my hidden talents
And spend time on myself
Beyond the labels of a mother and wife
A world where I have the freedom to make choices
Just like a man
A world where brides won't be persecuted for dowry
One in which there is no honor killing
By lofty fathers and brothers
A world where I can chose my mate
And express my desires to soar
A world that treats women like queens
Each day and not just one day out of 365
Yes I aspire for such a world today.

17. WOMAN

You were born a woman for a purpose
It is no accident for sure
You are here to deliver a story
Strong, real and pure
You skipped through mustard fields
Climbed the sprawling mango tree
Played house with your strawberry doll
And went gallivanting on market sprees
Your tender heart missed a beat
As you roamed rosy eyed focusing on your crush
You burnt the midnight oil for that degree
And your chosen path was no light brush
You walked around the sacred fire
Vowing to stand by your mate
A promise you made in all earnestness
That holds true till the evening late
You were blessed with motherhood
An experience that made you grow
You juggled the roles of wife and mother
Oh boy it was an incredible show
Suddenly the shadows loomed large
And ominous clouds gathered in front
You fought valiantly like the Goddess Kali

And your demeanor became bold and blunt
You carried your self esteem like Sita
Vowing to put things right like Draupadi
You garnered courage like the Goddess Durga
And put the equilibrium at ease
O woman you were born to bring glory
To the clan you were born into
You were also born to bring further glory
To the clan you chose to marry into
Let not the sparkle ever dull in your eyes
Like Saraswati may your speech never lose power
The world is yours for the taking and making
Salute your inner fire and let your grace shower

18. A SLICE OF HEAVEN

I have often wondered in awe
What would heaven be like
Is it a figment of human imagination?
Or a concrete thing of sight
I have often experienced blessings
Like the brilliant sheen of sunbeams
Enchanting melodies of the moon
On the darkest of charcoal nights
I have often paused and taken a break
To look up at the azure sky
Feel the infinite yonder blue
Flirting with cumulous clouds
I have often gone in raptures
At the tender folds of a rose
Enchanted by its heady fragrance
And marveled at the thorn its foe
I have often stood awe struck at the beach
Marveled at the sea shells at the shore
The relentless rising and falling of waves
Have assured me there is a heaven for sure
I have often wondered how you found me
In this chaotic infinite world

It was surely serendipity at best
When you glided with your aura indoors
But the most magical heaven of all
Lies in your deep brown eyes
And the voice that speaks to me in adoration
O, you are truly my slice of heaven on earth
The rendezvous was one of ecstatic heights
In a world of our very own
O how wondrous was the slice of heaven
A memory that smells like heaven for sure!

19. SO WHAT

Alas
Our Spring lasted fleetingly
A handful of moments
We gathered gleefully in our palms
Uncaring about tomorrow
Lost in the joy of union
Of ecstatic moments
Unable to believe
It was actually happening
Alas
Spring never gave way to joyful Summer
What came
Was the harsh winter of separation
Tearful and heart wrenching
But did we not continue our song
Albeit in hidden corridors of time?
Did we not continue to flourish
Despite being in different terrains?
Did we not cherish the memories
Day after day?
So what if Spring danced capriciously
It left tell tale songs of love
Etched deeply in our hearts

Replacing the ephemeral flowers
With pearls of life!

20. 57th MILESTONE

Is it really true?
That I have reached the 57th milestone?
Finally saying No to blues
And bidding a firm goodbye to moans
How wondrous has been the journey
Interspersed with darkness and light
O it was delightful to be around honey
And soak in the sunshine bright
Is it really true
That I am inching towards being a senior citizen
No matter what or who
It is now goodbye to times frozen
What a sojourn it has been
Meeting my fate and accepting the date
Endless drama I have seen
But ended up with affable mates
Is it really true that I am a little wise
Finally tearing apart the net of shroud
I sure have paid a hefty price
But boy, it has been worth it, I say aloud!
It is now time to chase away melancholy
And usher in all graces of life
Finally time to script a melodious story

That has no shadows of strife
It is now that I promise myself time for sweet Nature
And drown in the joy of music
Fill up my life with splendid features
And curate a pretty garden of vibrant Tulips
It is time for deeper truths of life
Banalities no longer interest me
No more complaints and mindless cries
It is time to be joyous and just be
I have studied the texts aplenty
And discussed tales too
It is finally time to introspect fully
And live at peace and in a manner true.
People do charities and so much more
I too get inspired by them for sure
The greatest gift I feel i can give at ease
Is by being humble, humane and a friend to thee

21. GLORY OF LIFE

Every now and then
The chaos in the jungle of life
Traps me in a web of cacophony
Impairing my hearing
Numbing my senses
Cutting me away from the glory of life
But life you surprise me
One day after the other
Like the vibrant plumes of the Macaws
Or the melodious singing of the Koel
Or the arrival of Spring after a dreary winter
Reminding me of the glory of life
When faced with machinations of some
You send saviors in hoods of redemption
Riding high on goodness and faith
Resurrecting me from the depths of despair
Surrounding me in a sea of hope
Shining the piercing rays of sunbeams
O life, how spellbinding is your eternal glory!

22. ODE TO SOPHIE

Soulful eyes
Or simply Sophie
You are such a delight
Since you came into our lives
You travelled all the way from Sonipat
To the welcoming lap of Surbhi
Who was the brain behind bringing you home
And the first person to cuddle you
O, how thrilling it was indeed
As we four went to the pet shop
To bring you home
In grand style
The girls put you in a basket
With pink ribbons and golden net
A befitting welcome gesture
Announced on Instagram
You were as delicate as a bird
And unsure of your surroundings
Yet you quickly learnt to call the blanket
Your home
We watched with utmost love
As you lapped up the feed of cerelac
Slowly graduating to eating starter

And everything from eggs, fruit and home food
We watched in wonder
As the tiny puppy with the strength of a bird
Changed into a confident puppy two months later
Doing the marathon between her two beds
In two bedrooms
Your pranks with socks and slippers
Your fights with shoes
And burying your face inside
Your trademark dance
When a visitor comes home
Your sneaking into the kitchen
To steal an empty packet of milk or curd
Your howling protests when locked in the verandah
To enable maids to do their chores
Your high jumps to catch food
Your escorting me into the bathroom and kitchen
And a host of other antics, hold us sway
You are such a stress buster
A power house of love
Licking away to glory
And gently biting with your canines
But perhaps the greatest lesson you have taught us is
Your faith in yourself
The way you have made our home your own
You are a true blessing
A darling of the Midha family

A Godsend
The most pampered member of our family
We love you SOPHIE
Wishing you a long and healthy life

23. THE LIGHT

Like a meteor
The light zoomed in
A celestial event
That was simply meant to be
Like a breath of fresh air
The light breezed
Spreading heady fragrance
Enchanting the mind
Like ripples of laughter
The faces burst into creases
Rolling with joy
Of shared moments
Like a delicious dish
With the secret ingredients
Titillating the taste buds
Filling up with contentment
Like a giant ferry wheel
The excitement was unending
The adrenalin rush inescapable
It was love after all
The unexpected parting
As the light shifted focus
Making its way to an eternal gift

Such was the magic of the light

24. MILESTONES

Long ago the fire burnt
Engulfing all the good
Destroying her joy to ashes
Covered with ash
She shrugged off the grey remains
Cleansed her mouth
Of the bitter taste
Vowing to break free
Like a phoenix she rose
From the very ashes of her tender heart
Gently wiping away the tears
As she welcomed the new dawn
Today she is a born again woman
Living a new life
Caressing every moment
Reveling in the cocoon like warmth
Today she is building memories
Having slayed the demons
Enjoying the milestones
She is you, she and every woman
INSPIRATION
O life you come galloping in a thousand hues
Filling me up with joy and enthusiasm on cue

Just when the going gets a little tough
You show beautifully life need not be rough
O life you bring inspiration in so many ways
Sometimes it is people and sometimes it is sunset days
The sheer beauty of human life
A million possibilities despite strife
O life you gather a cartload of memories
To browse and warm your heart with treasuries
Moments and celebrations from yore
Pushing me to love life even more
O life you inspire the mother in me
I want to give unconditionally and let this always be
There is joy inherent in motherhood
My heart skips a beat as I see my child in red hood
O life you made a poet of me
I can express emotions beautifully for all to see
What a joy to leave a legacy of thoughts and emotions behind
It will be a dazzling tale for all and remind.

25. INSPIRATION

26. ODE TO LOVE

Love the incredible emotion of life
Is born even when the baby is inside,
Vows to nurture empower and remove strife
The tender hands gathered when the baby cried.
The love of a teacher strict and benign
Teaching the values with a shining grace,
The love for a deity at the sacred shrine
Love forever promises to keep pace.
The love of a friend playful and naughty
Of childish pranks, dreams and adventures,
Nay, love is never haughty and pricey
Love aspires to fulfil the bond at all ventures.
The first crush and the raging fever
Of dreamy days and wriggly giggles,
The mating love of the diligent bird weaver
Oh, love need not be an enigma or a riddle.
The love for a spouse and years of living
Raising kids and a loving family,
Of festivals galore and happy thanksgiving
Love is indeed everyone's quest in the galaxy.
Ah, the rare deep love for a soul mate
Surpassing logic, reason and incredulity,
Blessed are those who meet their soul mate

For lovers, love is a splendid song musically.

27. @58

Here comes another year
Knocking at the door on my birthday
A wondrous feeling to shoo away fear
As a happy life is no longer at bay
The days of youth are way past
And tasks big and small have been deftly handled
A cartload of memories to last
And grudges and errors neatly bundled
This is the rainbow year
As I am happily retired from work
And now it is time for happy gear
And say goodbye to things that irk
Today there are no more blues
Life has taught many precious lessons
It is time to enjoy stories new
And an invitation of scripting happiness by pen
Thank you God, my precious benefactor
For this life and a brand new year
Living in the moment is the secret factor
Embracing a ripe life now and here
The world has been explored for all its beauty
The sermons no more enchant
Now it is really the comfort zone and duty

It's my life, is my heart's only chant.

28. HOLI

The two day festival of Holi
Is truly a festival of love, colors and Spring wholly
A festival welcoming Spring after winters
Where a myriad of colors take wings
Prahlad, the devout son of Asura king Hiranyakashapu
Never worshipped his father but Lord Vishnu
Angered the asura king set up a trap via his sister Holika
But the fireproof cloak of Holika flew onto Prahlad saving him
And Holika was burnt to ashes
The next day people celebrate with colors
Tesu, Neem, haldi, kumkum, beetroot
Now giving way to herbal gulal
Smearing color with joy and gaiety
Lord Vishnu took the form of Narasimha
Which was half man and half lion
Took Hiranyakashyapa at dawn on his lap
And killed him with his claws
And there is the tale of Krishna
The dark skinned Kanha woed to his mother
Will the fair skinned Radha accept me?
Yashodha advised Kanha to smear Radha's face with colors of his choice

And thus began a divine love story of Radha Krishna
The Braj region is famous for Holi
Especially Barsana, the town of Radha
Gopis and Gopas play mock lathmar Holi
And celebrate this festival with pranks
Holi is a celebration of end of winters
And the beginning of a Spring harvest
Sheaves of green wheat are roasted in the fire and partaken as prasad along with gujiya
But above all Holi stands for renewal, rebirth and harmony
Of forgiving, letting go and starting a new leaf
Let us drown in the ecstasy of Spring colors
Let us celebrate the festival of colors and triumph of good over evil

29. ALLURING WOMAN

You were born a woman for a purpose
It is no accident for sure
You are here to deliver a story
Strong, real and pure
You skipped through mustard fields
Climbed the sprawling mango tree
Played house with your strawberry doll
And went gallivanting on market sprees
Your tender heart missed a beat
As you roamed rosy eyed focusing on your crush
You burnt the midnight oil for that degree
And your chosen path was no light brush
You walked around the sacred fire
Vowing to stand by your mate
A promise you made in all earnestness
That holds true till the evening late
You were blessed with motherhood
An experience that made you grow
You juggled the roles of wife and mother
Oh boy it was an incredible show
Suddenly the shadows loomed large
And ominous clouds gathered in front

You fought valiantly like the Goddess Kali
And your demeanor became bold and blunt
You carried your self esteem like Sita
Vowing to put things right like Draupadi
You garnered courage like the Goddess Durga
And put the equilibrium at ease
O woman you were born to bring glory
To the clan you were born into
You were also born to bring further glory
To the clan you chose to marry into
Let not the sparkle ever dull in your eyes
Like Saraswati may your speech never lose power
The world is yours for the taking and making
Salute your inner fire and let your grace shower

30. ODE TO POETRY

Seven years ago on World Poetry Day
I became a published poet for sure
Leaving every trace of melancholy at bay
Feelings poured into poems as emotions pure
Oh what a journey of composing it has been
From pet Sophie to love and a dozen other dreams
The sheer joy of penning down things seen
From the merry circus clown to the fairy queen
Several poetry books I celebrate today
Harmony, Home Alone, Yesterday Once More to name a few
Composing poems became the sure shot way
From falling raindrops to tender morning dew
Immortalizing people and incidents was the aim
Rhymes or free verse whatever came my way
The sheer joy of sharing poems with friends
There was so much to do and seemingly no end
Today it has been seven glorious years
Of living as a poet and connoisseur for sure
I thank one and all of my poetry peers
Without you the journey would never have geared.

Printed by Libri Plureos GmbH in Hamburg, Germany